Us ~~IBRARIES~~ s

Sea & Freshwater
Birds

Joe Blossom

Illustrated by Trevor Boyer,
Alan Harris & Ian Jackson

Consultant: Peter Holden

Usborne Quicklinks

The Usborne Quicklinks Website is packed with thousands of links to all the best websites on the internet. The websites include information, video clips, sounds, games and animations that support and enhance the information in Usborne internet-linked books.

To visit the recommended websites for Spotter's Sea and Freshwater Birds, go to the Usborne Quicklinks Website at **www.usborne-quicklinks.com** and enter the keywords: **spotters sea birds**

Internet safety

When using the internet please follow the internet safety guidelines displayed on the Usborne Quicklinks Website. The recommended websites in Usborne Quicklinks are regularly reviewed and updated, but Usborne Publishing Ltd is not responsible for the content or availability of any website other than its own. We recommend that children are supervised while using the internet.

Usborne Publishing is not responsible and does not accept liability for the availability or content of any website other than its own, or for any exposure to harmful, offensive, or inaccurate material which may appear on the Web. Usborne Publishing will have no liability for any damage or loss caused by viruses that may be downloaded as a result of browsing the sites it recommends.

Contents

How to use this book

This guide will help you identify birds that live on or near water. Sea birds are found near the salty water at the coast. You'll find freshwater birds further inland, for example near rivers, lakes, reservoirs and flooded gravel pits.

In this book, birds that are usually found near fresh water are shown on pages 10-36; the seabirds are on pages 37-52. Birds that look similar have been grouped together, to make it easier to find the one you're looking for. Here's an example of the descriptions you'll find in the guide:

Name

◀ **Spoonbill**

Description

Rarely nests, but a regular visitor to east and southwest England. Likes shallow fresh or coastal water. Breeds in southern Europe. 86cm

Length, including beak and tail

Male and female

The males and females of some species can look different from each other. The symbols male ♂ and female ♀ show you which is which.

Shovelers
♀

♂

4

Areas covered

The dark green area of this map shows the part of the world covered in the guide. Not every bird that lives in this area has been included, and the ones that have are not always very widely spread. If they are rare in Britain, their description will tell you in which part of the country to find them.

Iceland

Scandinavia

The British Isles

Mainland Europe

Keeping a record

There's an empty circle next to each picture. Whenever you spot a bird for the first time, you can put a tick in the circle.

Scorecard

There's a scorecard at the end of the book that gives an idea of how common each bird is. You score 5 points for ones that are easy to spot, and 25 for ones that are most difficult.

You can fill in the scorecard like this

Species (name)	Score	Spotted
Kingfisher	20	
Kittiwake	15	Farne Islands
Knot	15	2nd Dec
Lapwing	10	

Spotting birds

When you're out in the country looking for birds, it's a good idea to wear a sturdy pair of waterproof boots to keep your feet warm and dry. Some birds nest on cliffs – take care not to go too near the edge.

Birds will fly off if you get too close, so the best way to see them clearly is through a pair of binoculars. Ones with a magnification of 8×30 or 8×40 will give you a good view, without being too heavy to hold steady.

PARTS OF A BIRD

When you train your binoculars on a bird that's standing still, you'll be able to see all these parts of its body clearly.

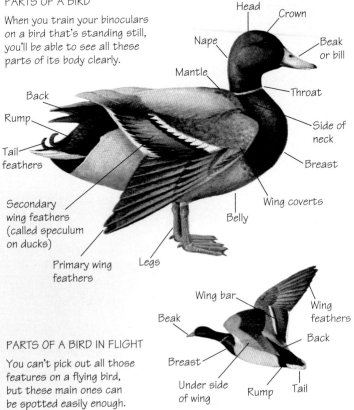

Head
Crown
Nape
Beak or bill
Mantle
Throat
Back
Side of neck
Rump
Breast
Tail feathers
Wing coverts
Secondary wing feathers (called speculum on ducks)
Belly
Primary wing feathers
Legs

PARTS OF A BIRD IN FLIGHT

You can't pick out all those features on a flying bird, but these main ones can be spotted easily enough.

Wing bar
Wing feathers
Beak
Back
Breast
Under side of wing
Rump
Tail

6

Making notes

If you see a bird that's not in this guide, you can make notes and sketches to help you identify it from other books, or the internet. Here's a list of features that are useful to note down:

• What size is it? Compare it to a bird you know.
• What are its colours? Look at feathers, beak, legs.

• Where and when did you see it? Birds live in particular places, and some are in the country for only part of the year.
• What's it doing? Maybe it's diving for food, pecking for seeds or nesting in a colony.

This sketch shows the sort of notes you might make

June 22nd, Shingleton Beach

Smaller than a starling

Hopping along the shingle

White belly

Black 'v' on wings

Stubby tail

Part of a small flock

Feeding

Sea birds

Sea ducks such as Eiders find food on the seabed near the shore.

Cormorants dive after fish using their feet to propel them.

Auks and Razorbills dive for fish using their wings and feet to propel them.

Waders

Waders live on estuaries (where rivers flow into the sea) and probe the mud for food. They feed at different depths, depending on the shape of their beak, which varies from short and stubby to long and curved.

Turnstones look under pebbles for small animals.

Ringed Plovers seek small snails on the surface of the mud.

Knots (left) and Redshanks probe the mud for shrimps and ragworms.

Wildfowl

Greylag Geese have heavy bills for breaking into soft roots.

Teal dabble for seeds at the water's edge.

Barnacle Geese graze on grass in saltmarshes.

Gannets and Terns plunge headfirst into water from flight.

Gulls skim food from the surface.

Skuas chase other sea birds such as Terns, to make them drop their fish.

Oystercatchers use their tough, pointed beaks to prise open cockles and other shellfish.

Bar-tailed Godwits (left) and Curlews probe the mud for Lugworms, Ragworms and deeper-living shellfish.

Bewick's Swans reach into deeper water for underwater weeds.

Shovelers sieve seeds and small animals from the water's surface.

Pochards feed mainly on plants in deeper water. They dive to reach them.

Mallards (left) and Pintails "upend" for seeds, plants and small water animals.

9

Swans

⬇ Mute Swan

Parks or rivers are the best places to see Mute Swans. Look for their huge mounded nest on small islands in fresh water and marshes. They feed on deep-lying plants by plunging their head into the water. Normally silent but, if irritated, hiss or give a sharp snort. 1.52m

All swan species fly with outstretched necks

Wing beats make a regular swishing-whistling sound

Juveniles keep some grey-brown plumage until they are two years old

Adults have orange bill with black knob

Neck curved in an S-shape

The downy young of all swan species are called cygnets

These cygnets are swimming next to their parent, but sometimes they get carried on its back.

➡ Bewick's Swan

The smallest swan, with the shortest neck. The pattern of its black and yellow bill varies. Breeds in the Russian Arctic. Most spend winter in southern half of Britain and Ireland. 1.22m

Juvenile

About one third of the bill is yellow

Neck is always straight when held up

➡ Whooper Swan

Has longer neck and beak than Bewick's Swan. Bill is more yellow than black. Like all swans, seen on lakes, rivers, estuaries and sheltered water on coast. Most migrate from Iceland to spend winter in Scotland and northern England. 1.52m

Yellow area comes to a point

Upper neck straight, lower part near body often bent

Geese

Short black bill with pink band

← Pink-footed Goose

Look for this small, dark goose on northern estuaries in winter. From a distance, the head and neck look very dark. 68cm

Pink legs

→ Bean Goose

A rare winter visitor from northern Europe. Grazes on farmland away from the coast. 80cm

Orange and black bill

Orange legs

Heavy bill

← Greylag Goose

Lives all year round on lakes, reservoirs, and gravel pits in England. Winter visitor to Scotland from Iceland. 82cm

➡ Lesser White-fronted Goose

Very rare but regular winter visitor. Usually lives in flocks with European White-fronted Goose. Feeds more quickly than the European. 60cm

Pink bill

Yellow eye-ring

More white on crown than European White-fronted Goose

Orange legs

European and Greenland White-fronted Geese are different races of the same species

⬅ European White-fronted Goose

Winter migrant from Russia. Spends winter in southern England. All adult White-fronted Geese have barring on their belly. 71cm

European race has pink bill and orange legs

➡ Greenland White-fronted Goose

Spends winters in Ireland and western Scotland. A darker bird than the European, with heavier belly markings. 72cm

Greenland race has orange bill and orange legs

Geese

➡ Snow Goose

A rare visitor from North America. Has two colour variations: white and blue. Both are usually seen amongst flocks of other geese. 68cm

"White" Snow Goose

"Blue" Snow Goose

Very small, short bill

The Red-breasted is the smallest goose

⬅ Red-breasted Goose

Very rare winter visitor from the Russian Arctic. Look for it in flocks with White-fronted or Brent Geese. 54cm

More white on head than Canada Goose

➡ Barnacle Goose

Seen on the west coasts of Britain and Ireland in winter. Feeds in flocks on farmland. 63cm

← Canada Goose

Large goose with loud, honking call. Introduced to Britain 300 years ago. Now common on inland lakes, parks and reservoirs. Up to 95cm

➡ Brent Goose (Dark-bellied race)

Lives on estuaries and mudflats on south and east coasts of Britain in winter. Small for a goose – about the same size as a Mallard. 58cm

Adults of both types of Brent have a white collar

Dark belly

← Brent Goose (Light-bellied race)

A winter visitor from the Arctic Circle. Seen on mudflats in northeast England and Ireland. 58cm

Light belly

Eel grass

15

Estuary ducks

Female has no lump on bill ♀

♂

Male is called sheldrake

← Shelduck

Common around most sandy coasts, especially estuaries. Sometimes nests in rabbit holes. Often seen in flocks. Looks slow and heavy in flight. 61cm

➡ Wigeon

Sometimes seen grazing on fields near water. Forms flocks in winter, especially near the sea. Male's call is a loud "wheeo". 46cm

♀

Drake has bright yellow forehead

♂

Wigeon are often seen grazing on fields near water

➡ American Wigeon

Rare visitor, mostly seen in Ireland in winter. Greyer and less colourful than Wigeon. Drake's forehead cream rather than yellow. 47cm

♀

♂

Diving ducks

← Scaup

Winter visitor to bays and estuaries. Similar to Tufted Duck, but drake has grey back, and female has more white at base of beak. 48cm

→ Tufted Duck

Another diving duck which is more common in winter. Can sometimes be seen on park lakes. 43cm

Tuft

Peak

Peak

← Ring-necked Duck

Rare visitor from North America. Very similar to Tufted Duck but has peak, not tuft, on top of head. Female has white eye-ring and white near bill. 43cm

→ Goldeneye

A few nest in Scotland, but mainly a winter visitor from northern Europe. Seen on the sea and inland lakes. Dives frequently. 46cm

17

Diving ducks

♀ ♂

← Pochard

Spends most of its time resting on lowland lakes and reservoirs. Dives to feed on water plants. More likely to be seen in winter. 46cm

You can tell a Pochard drake from a Wigeon by its pure chestnut head and neck, and black breast

→ Red-crested Pochard

Rare visitor from southern Europe. Seen mostly in eastern England. Its white hindwing shows in flight. 55cm

Duck (female) has pale cheek

♀ ♂

Drake has red bill and red legs

♀ ♂

White under tail

← Ferruginous Duck

Breeds in southern and eastern Europe. Occasionally seen in Britain on fresh water with other diving ducks, mainly in winter. 40cm

Sawbills

All these ducks have a saw-edged bill for gripping live fish.

Both duck and drake have crests

♀

♂

← Red-breasted Merganser

Breeds by lakes and rivers. Seldom seen inland in winter, but visits many coastal areas and open sea. Dives for fish. 58cm

→ Goosander

Most British Goosanders nest in the north and west. Favours fast-flowing streams and rivers in summer, and lakes and reservoirs in winter. 66cm

Only female has shaggy crest

♀

♂

→ Smew

Occasional winter visitor to southern England. Breeds by fresh water in forests in northern Europe. Males and females often seen separately. 41cm

♀

♂

Sea ducks

Cheek and front of neck are pale

♀

♂

← Common Scoter

Mainly seen during winter on coastal water, especially in southern and eastern England. Often in flocks. 46cm

→ Velvet Scoter

Look for this winter visitor on coastal waters. Often with Common Scoters or Eiders. White secondary feathers are visible in flight. 56cm

Two pale patches on head

♀

White "tear" shape around eye

♂

♀

♂

Male has large, multi-coloured bill

← Surf Scoter

Regular but rare visitor from North America to coastal waters. No white wing bar in flight. Female very similar to Velvet, with extra nape patch. 50cm

➡ Eider

Fast-flying duck that breeds near seashores in northern Britain and northern Europe. Seen further south in winter, off rocky or sandy coasts. Soft downy feathers taken from its nest after the young have hatched are used to stuff pillows and duvets. 58cm

⬅ King Eider

This very rare winter visitor breeds in the Arctic. A huge, orange forehead makes the drake unmistakable. Female usually a redder brown than Eider duck. 56cm

➡ Long-tailed Duck

Breeds in the Arctic and also in some mountains in Scandinavia. Many spend winter around British coasts, very occasionally on inland reservoirs. Drake 53cm. Duck 41cm

Both sexes have more black on head in summer

Winter

Winter

Dabbling ducks

➡ Mallard

The most common wildfowl. Look for it on still and slow-moving water. Lives in Britain all year round. Often breeds with other kinds of duck – most farmyard ducks are descended from Mallards. Only the female gives the famous "quack". 58cm

Drakes chase females as the breeding season approaches

Nest covered in downy feathers

Mallard drake in "eclipse plumage" during its moult, after the breeding period in summer. It looks similar to the female, but look for olive-green bill.

♂

Like all wildfowl young, mallard ducklings hatch with eyes open and leave the nest quickly

♀

Blue speculum

♂

➡ Shoveler

Uses its heavy bill to sieve food from surface of water. Seen inland and on coast. You can see its shovel-shaped bill even in flight. 51cm

♀

♂

Both sexes show blue forewing in flight.

Looks similar to Mallard but speculum is black and white

♀

⬅ Gadwall

Quite scarce. Breeds mainly in eastern Britain and most often seen in winter. Found on lowland marshes and lakes. 51cm

♂

Dark rear

White stripe runs up neck of male

Long slender neck

Female has pointed tail

➡ Pintail

Uses its long neck to feed on underwater plants. Look for these birds in winter, often near the sea. Flies very fast. Drake 66cm. Duck 56cm

♂

♀

Male has very long tail feathers

Dabbling ducks

♀ ♂

➡ Garganey

Seen in summer. Breeds near shallow water, mainly in eastern England. White stripe over drake's eye. 38cm

➡ Teal

Smallest European duck. A very shy bird. It prefers the shallow edges of lakes. Flies with fast wing beats. 35cm

♀ ♂

➡ Green-winged Teal

A rare visitor. Has white stripe on side of breast. 35cm

♂

➡ Blue-winged Teal

Rare but regular visitor from North America. The pale blue on its wings shows in flight. 38cm

♂ ♀

➡ Marbled Teal

One of the rarest ducks to breed in Europe. Seen in summer in southern Spain and France. Male and female look alike. 41cm

Perching ducks, Stifftails

➡ Mandarin Duck

Introduced from China. Several small wild populations in southern Britain. Nests in tree holes. 46cm

⬅ Carolina Duck

Introduced from North America. Nests in tree holes. Perches on branches. 48cm

➡ Ruddy Duck

Originally from North America. Now lives wild in England and southern Scotland. In courtship display male beats chest, making cloud of bubbles. 39cm

⬅ White-headed Duck

The European counterpart of Ruddy Duck. Now a rare breeding bird in southern Europe. Not usually wild in Britain. 45cm

Rails

← Moorhen

Lives and breeds on any small area of water. Shy in the wild, but can become tame in parks. Sometimes nests on garden ponds. 33cm

Red bill with yellow tip

White shield

→ Coot

Usually seen on lakes and reservoirs. Adult birds have white shield on forehead. Dives to feed on water plants. 38cm

Legs trail out in flight, as do legs of Moorhen and Coot

← Water Rail

Secretive bird that lives in reed beds. Listen for its piglet-like squeals and grunts. Swims for short distances. 28cm

Barring on belly

Divers, Grebe

➡ Red-throated Diver

The most commonly seen diver. Breeds in the Scottish Highlands near fresh water. Spends winter at sea. 56cm

Winter

Summer

⬅ Black-throated Diver

Winter

Breeds in the Scottish Highlands near large areas of freshwater. Spends winter at sea. Call is a loud wailing cry. 60cm

Summer

➡ Great Northern Diver

Only once nested in Britain. Seen in winter on coasts, when its head is black. 75cm

Winter

Summer

⬅ Great Crested Grebe

Crest expands during display

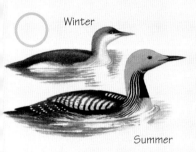

Summer

Winter

Found on lakes and reservoirs. Also on coast in winter. Dives for fish. Elaborate courtship displays in spring. 48cm

Grebes

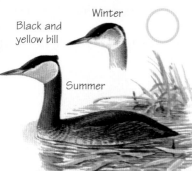

Winter

Summer

Chestnut cheeks and throat

◀ Little Grebe or Dabchick

Common on inland waters, but secretive and hard to spot. Call is a shrill trill. 27cm

➡ Slavonian Grebe

Regular winter visitor to coasts. In winter looks similar to Black-necked Grebe, but note crown and straight bill. 33cm

Winter

Summer

Black and yellow bill

Winter

Summer

◀ Red-necked Grebe

Look for it by the coast in winter. Similar to Great Crested Grebe, but has black and yellow bill, and dark crown. 43cm

Winter

Upturned bill

Summer

➡ Black-necked Grebe

Breeds in a few places in Britain. Mainly winter visitor. Similar to Slavonian, but has a deeper crown and upturned bill. 30cm

Spoonill, Flamingo

➡ Spoonbill

Rarely nests, but
a regular visitor to
east and southwest
England. Likes shallow
fresh or coastal water.
Breeds in southern
Europe. 86cm

Has yellow breast
in breeding season

Tip of bill
shaped
like spoon

Sometimes seen
stretching one wing

Ankles

Wings are red and
black in flight

The Chilean race is
sometimes seen after
escaping from wildfowl
collections. It has grey
legs with red ankles
and feet.

⬅ Greater Flamingo

Seen in parts of southern
Europe, often in large,
noisy groups. Lives on
shallow lakes. Uses its
curved bill to sieve food
from water. Builds cone-
shaped nests from mud.
Juveniles have grey-
brown plumage. 127cm

Storks

➡ White Stork

A very rare but
regular visitor to
Britain. Seen
mainly in summer
in eastern Europe and
Spain. Lives on marshes
and farmland. Feeds on
insects, frogs and small
mammals. 110cm

*Storks stretch out
their necks and trail
their legs when they fly*

⬅ Black Stork

Has been known to visit
Britain, but very rarely.
Seen in summer mainly in
eastern Europe. Lives in
and near forests. Feeds at
the edges of fresh water
and on marshes. Juveniles
have browner plumage,
especially on head and
neck. 100cm

*All black
with white
underparts*

Crane, Heron

➡ Crane

Mostly breeds in Scandinavia and northern Europe, although there is a small population in eastern England. Lives on bogs, marshes and wet heaths. Never lands in trees. Feeds on land. 112cm

Flies with neck outstretched and legs trailing. Migrates in lines or v-formation.

Both sexes have black "eyebrow" stripe and crest

Heron flies with head drawn back and legs trailing

➡ Grey Heron

A very common freshwater bird. Nests in colonies in trees. Feeds on fish, frogs and small mammals. 92cm

Herons

← Night Heron

A rare visitor to Britain, but one colony lives wild in Scotland, at Edinburgh Zoo. Found on marshes in southern Europe in summer. Hunts at night. 70cm

Black crown

Reddish neck with black stripes

Black belly

→ Purple Heron

May be seen on migration in Britain, particularly in eastern England. Favours marshes and reed beds. A shyer bird than Grey Heron. 78cm

Often hunches up its neck

← Bittern

Rare in Britain. Breeds mainly in east England. Lives in reed beds. Sticks its neck up when alarmed Has a booming call like a cow's "moo". 76cm

Heron, Egrets

➡ Squacco Heron

Has occasionally visited
Britain on migration.
Otherwise seen in southern
Europe, mainly in summer.
Lives on marshes. 45cm

⬅ Great White Egret

Seen very rarely in Britain.
Lives in south-eastern Europe,
on marshes and lakes. Long
plumes on back when
breeding. 95cm

Black
legs

➡ Little Egret

Lives mainly on south and
east coast of Britain, on
marshes and shallow water.
Flies with neck bent and
legs straight, like all herons
and egrets. 55cm

Two plumes
on head in
breeding
season

Black
legs and
yellow
feet

Kingfisher, Wagtail, Dipper

➡ Kingfisher

This small and
brilliantly coloured
bird lives near lakes and
rivers. Usually perches
near water before diving
for fish. Listen for its shrill,
piping call. 16cm

Often flies low
and straight
over water

Often seen wagging its
very long tail up and down

Summer

♂

⬅ Grey Wagtail

Usually nests near
fast-flowing mountain
streams. Paler in winter,
when it visits lowland
waters. Catches insects
in flight. 18cm

Northern
Europe

Britain and
Central Europe

Has no
reddish-brown
underparts

➡ Dipper

Seen by fast-flowing
mountain streams. Walks
underwater to find food.
Bobs up and down.
Breeds in north and
west Britain. 18cm

Reddish-brown
underparts

Bunting, Warblers, Harrier

➡ Reed Bunting

Usually found in marshy places, reed beds and near fresh water. Flicks tail while perching. 15cm

♀

♂

Reddish rump shows in flight

⬅ Sedge Warbler

Spends most of its time in thick vegetation near fresh water. Summer only in Britain. 13cm

➡ Reed Warbler

Summer visitor to southern Britain. Nests in the middle of reed beds. Nest is attached to reeds. 12.5cm

♂

⬅ Marsh Harrier

In Britain, nests mainly in east England in reed beds and marshes. Sweeps low over the ground with slow wing beats. 52cm

♀

Birds of prey

➡ Osprey

Summer visitor to Britain.
Breeds in Scotland, north
England and Wales.
Plunges into water
to catch fish. 56cm

Strong claws
for gripping
slippery fish

Varies from
dark to light
grey on top

Black streak
on cheek a
different shape
on each bird

◀ Peregrine

Breeds on sea cliffs,
mountain crags and
some buildings. Hunts
over estuaries and
coastal marshes in
winter. Dives on flying
birds at enormous
speed. 39-50cm

➡ White-tailed
Sea Eagle

Britain's largest bird of
prey. Very rare. Breeds
on the west coast of
Scotland and Hebrides.
Feeds on sea birds and
fish. 68-97cm

Has very
broad wings

Adult has short
white tail

Gulls

➡ Black-headed Gull

Very common gull. Seen
as often inland as on
coast. Nests in colonies on
marshes, dunes, shingle.
Head is only dark in
summer. 38cm

Winter

Pale edge
to wing

Summer

Orange-
yellow legs

⬅ Lesser Black-backed Gull

Mainly a summer visitor,
though some spend winter
in Britain. Similar to Herring
Gull but look out for its much
darker grey back. 55cm

➡ Greater Black-backed Gull

Britain's largest gull. Not
often seen inland. Nests on
rocky coasts. Usually seen
in ones or twos. Back is
blacker than Lesser Black-
backed Gull's. 70cm

Pinkish
legs

Gulls

◀ Herring Gull

Common in ports and seaside towns. Scrounges food from people. Nests on buildings. Will drop shellfish from a height to open them. 62cm

➡ Common Gull

Can be confused with Kittiwake so check colour of the legs. Some nest in Scotland and Ireland. Look out for it further south, and inland, in winter. 40cm

Yellow legs

Black legs

◀ Kittiwake

Nests in colonies on cliffs. Lives out at sea when not breeding. Often seen following ships. 43cm

Terns

Bill is
all red

Arctic
Tern

Bill has
black tip

Common
Tern

← Arctic Tern
← Common Tern

Arctics seen mainly by northern coasts in Britain. Commons seen more in the south, often inland. Dives for fish. 34cm

➡ Black Tern

Mainly a spring and autumn visitor. Can be seen flying low over lakes, dipping down to pick food from the surface. 24cm

Summer

Autumn

White
forehead

Yellow
bill with
black tip

Orange-
yellow
legs

← Little Tern

Summer visitor. Nests in small groups on shingle beaches. Has loud call and very fast wing beats. Often hovers before diving for fish. 24cm

➡ Sandwich Tern

Seen on coasts in summer. Flies high with deep wing beats. Much larger than the species of tern shown above. 41cm

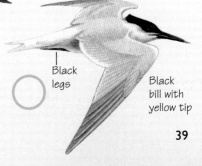

Black
legs

Black
bill with
yellow tip

Skuas, Fulmar

➡ Great Skua

A large, heavy-looking bird, often seen out at sea. Some breed in northern Scotland on cliff-tops and moorland. Like all skuas, chases other sea birds to steal their food. 58cm

White patches on wings show in flight

"Dark" Arctic Skua (not shown) is brown all over

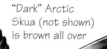

⬅ Arctic Skua

Seen along the coast, also breeding in northern Scotland. Same size as a Black-headed Gull. Has two colour variations: dark and pale. 50cm

Looks rather like Herring Gull but has no black wing tips

➡ Fulmar

Lives out at sea except during breeding season. Nests in colonies on sea cliffs all round Britain. Looks similar to a gull, but glides close to the waves on stiff wings. 47cm

Sits, never stands, on land

Shearwater, Petrels

← Manx Shearwater

All dark above, white underneath

Seen out at sea. Lands only to breed. Builds nest in burrow on island. Visits at night to avoid gulls. 35cm

May be seen in flocks at dusk, waiting to land at breeding ground

→ Storm Petrel

Seen at sea flying low over water. Follows ships. Smallest European sea bird, same size as a House Sparrow. Breeds on rocky islands in Scotland and Ireland. 15cm

Pale line on underwing

White rump

← Leach's Petrel

Looks similar to Storm Petrel, but note dark underwing. Has zigzag flight. Does not follow ships. Mostly seen in winter out at sea. 20cm

Dark underwing

Forked tail difficult to see in flight

Auks

Summer

Neck and throat are white in winter

➡ Razorbill

Nests in colonies on cliffs and rocky shores. Spends winter at sea. Dives for fish. Its flat-sided bill makes it easy to distinguish from other auks. 41cm

➡ Guillemot

The most commonly seen auk. Nests on cliff ledges in large, noisy groups. Some northern birds have a white eye ring and white line on their heads. 42cm

Neck and throat are white in winter

Summer

➡ Black Guillemot

Black in summer, with white wing patch. In winter turns white on lower parts, barred black and white on top. Bright red legs. 35cm

Summer

Summer

Brightly coloured bill in summer

➡ Puffin

Lives far out at sea. Breeds in burrows on grassy cliff tops and islands. Swims like a duck and dives to catch fish. 30cm

Cormorants, Gannet

← Shag

Lives on rocky coasts.
Nests in colonies. Dives
for fish, like all cormorants.
Crest is seen only in the
breeding season. Young
are brown. 76cm

← Gannet

Look for Gannets out
at sea, close to the
water. Dives headfirst
from a height to catch
fish. Nests on rocky
coasts. Young are
browner. 91cm

↓ Cormorant

Seen near the sea but
also inland on lakes.
Nests in colonies on
rocky ledges, or in
trees inland.
90cm

Often perches
and stretches
wings to dry in
the sun

Has white
thigh patch
in breeding
season

Waders

Winter

White collar
in winter

Summer

White wing
bars show
in flight

➡ Oystercatcher

Usually seen near the
sea, especially in winter.
Nests inland in Scotland
and parts of England.
Uses bill to open shellfish.
Listen for its piping call in
breeding season. 43cm

➡ Avocet

The only wader
with an upturned bill.
Breeds mainly on coastal
marshes in eastern England.
Some spend winter on
estuaries in southern
England. 43cm

Long pink
legs

Summer

⬅ Black-winged Stilt

Rare summer visitor to
Britain. Favours salt-marshes
and estuaries. Longest
legged of all waders. Legs
trail behind in flight. 38cm

← Ringed Plover

Usually found near the sea, but sometimes by inland lakes. Likes sandy or shingle shores. Seen all year round. 19cm

Juvenile

Summer

Broad white bar on wing

Wing bar rarely shows in flight

Summer

← Little Ringed Plover

Summer visitor. Gravel pits and shingle banks inland near fresh water. Has less black on forehead than Ringed Plover, and thinner, blacker beak. Also has yellow eye ring. 15cm

➡ Kentish Plover

Rare southern visitor. Seen on sand or shingle, usually on coast of southern Europe. Slimmer than Ringed Plovers, with longer, blacker legs. 16cm

Reddish-brown on crown

Black band does not form a complete ring.

Black legs

Waders

➜ Golden Plover

Breeds on upland moors, but found in flocks on coastal marshes or lowland farms in winter. 28cm

Northern Europe

Southern Europe

Winter

➜ Grey Plover

Winter visitor to eastern and southern coasts of Britain. Seen in small groups, mixed with other waders. 28cm

Summer

Winter

Summer

⬅ Turnstone

Likes shingle or rocky shores. Turns stones over to find food. Does not nest in Britain, but can be seen most months. 23cm

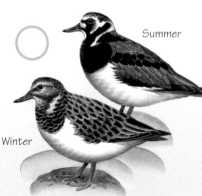

Winter

← Knot

A winter visitor from the Arctic. Forms spectacular flocks on sand or mudflats in estuaries. Rare inland. 25cm

Straight black bill

Winter

Short pale legs

→ Dunlin

Common wader forming flocks on seashores in winter. Nests on moorland in northern Britain. Northern birds bigger than southern. 17-19cm

Winter

White wing bar

Black belly in summer

Summer

Winter

← Sanderling

Mainly seen on migration in spring and autumn. Runs along water's edge on sandy beaches, catching small animals washed up by the waves. 20cm

Waders

➡ Lapwing

Present all year. Forms large flocks in winter on farmland, estuaries and mudflats. Looks black and white from a distance. Calls "pee-wit". 30cm

Broad rounded wings

Crest

⬅ Common Sandpiper

Summer visitor to upland streams and lakes. Visits wet areas in lowland Britain in spring and autumn. Wags its tail and bobs up and down. 20cm

Summer

➡ Purple Sandpiper

Winter visitor that also passes through in autumn and spring. Seen mainly on rocky shores. Nests on border of Arctic Circle in summer. 21cm

Winter

◀ Redshank

Common resident on the coast and on some wet meadows inland in summer. Look for its white rump, and listen for the loud "tew, tew" call. 28cm

Red legs

White hind wing

➡ Spotted Redshank

Seen mostly in autumn on migration. Prefers sea and estuary shores. Look for its wedge-shaped white rump. Has no white wing border. 30cm

Its white rump shows in flight

Winter

Summer

Greenshank has no white on wing

In flight, legs trail out further than Greenshank's or Redshank's

◀ Greenshank

Rarer and larger than Redshank. Seen in spring and autumn on coasts or inland. Some nest in northern Scotland. 30cm

Waders

➡ Red-necked Phalarope

A few breed on Scottish islands, but most likely to be seen on migration. In winter plumage very similar to Grey Phalarope's. 17cm

♀

♂

Summer

Summer

♂

♀

♀

Winter

⬅ Grey Phalarope

Like Red-necked Phalarope, female is more brightly coloured than male during summer. Males sit on eggs and rear young. Seen swimming on coastal pools. 20cm

White wing bar

Long legs

Summer

Summer

Winter

➡ Black-tailed Godwit

A few nest in wet meadows in Britain, but mostly seen on coasts during autumn and winter. 41cm

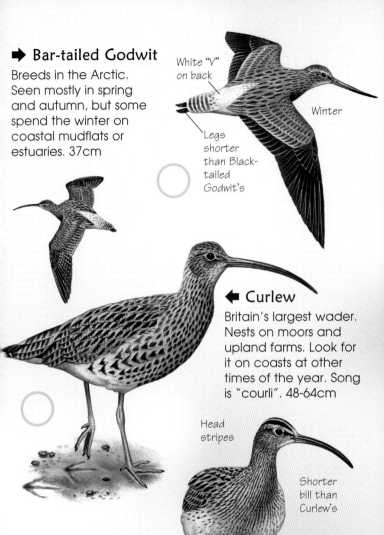

➡ Bar-tailed Godwit

Breeds in the Arctic. Seen mostly in spring and autumn, but some spend the winter on coastal mudflats or estuaries. 37cm

White "V" on back

Winter

Legs shorter than Black-tailed Godwit's

⬅ Curlew

Britain's largest wader. Nests on moors and upland farms. Look for it on coasts at other times of the year. Song is "courli". 48-64cm

Head stripes

Shorter bill than Curlew's

➡ Whimbrel

Like a small Curlew. A few nest in heather in northern Scotland. Many more visit Britain's coasts in spring and autumn. 40cm

51

Waders

♀

← Ruff

Seen mainly in spring
and autumn, but some
spend winter in wet
areas. Male's summer
plumage of ruff and
ear tufts varies in colour.
Female 23cm. Male 29cm

♂

Winter

♂

Summer

→ Woodcock

Secretive bird of damp
woodlands. Feeds usually
at night on marshy ground.
Watch out for its display
flight over woods at dusk
in early summer. 34cm

← Snipe

Lives in wet fields,
marshes or lake edges.
Hard to see on the
ground, but rises up with
a zigzag flight when
disturbed. 27cm

Migration

Many of the birds living around you have come from thousands of miles away. Some fly in from Africa each spring to lay their eggs and rear their young. Others fly down from the Arctic Circle in autumn.

Birds migrate from one place to another when their food begins to run out. They instinctively know where to go, and find their way using the Sun, the stars, and the Earth's magnetic field. If they've made the journey before they also look out for familiar landmarks.

Arctic Circle

Whatever time of year it is, you can spot birds that spend half the seasons on another side of the planet.

Europe

Bewick's Swans migrate south from the Arctic Circle in winter.

Some birds, such as Sanderlings, use Britain as a stop off point on their way south.

Africa

Every spring, White Storks migrate from southern Africa to their breeding grounds in central Europe.

Looking at feathers

Picking up a moulted feather is probably the closest you'll get to touching a wild bird. You'll see them on the ground in spring and summer, and if you look closely, you'll find there are four common shapes.

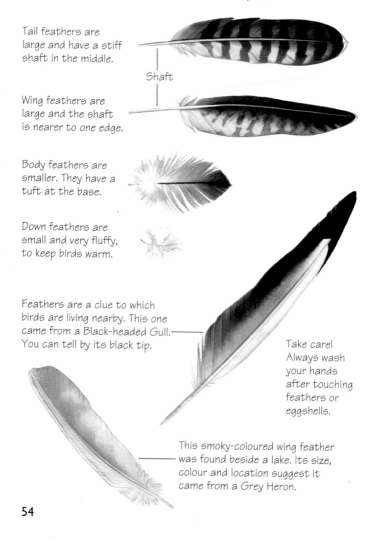

Tail feathers are large and have a stiff shaft in the middle.

Shaft

Wing feathers are large and the shaft is nearer to one edge.

Body feathers are smaller. They have a tuft at the base.

Down feathers are small and very fluffy, to keep birds warm.

Feathers are a clue to which birds are living nearby. This one came from a Black-headed Gull. You can tell by its black tip.

Take care! Always wash your hands after touching feathers or eggshells.

This smoky-coloured wing feather was found beside a lake. Its size, colour and location suggest it came from a Grey Heron.

Looking at eggshells

In spring and summer, broken eggshells lie half-buried in the sand, or long grass by rivers and lakes. Sometimes the chicks have hatched and left the shell behind, but it could be evidence of a hungry egg-thief at work.

Birds that nest on the ground lay camouflaged eggs. This Eider Duck eggshell blends in with the grass and kept its chick safe.

Despite mimicking the pebbles around it, this Oystercatcher eggshell was found by a gull, and its chick was eaten.

These hatched shells were laid by a Sandwich Tern. All birds that nest in groups lay eggs that are easily recognizable, so they don't get lost in the crowd.

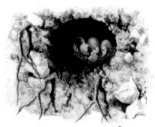

Birds that nest in holes lay pale eggs that stand out in the gloom. This riverbank Kingfisher nest has been plundered by a weasel.

The eggs of some cliff-nesting birds, like this Guillemot, are pointed at one end. If knocked they roll in a tight circle, instead of over the edge.

Bird silhouettes

Looking at its outline is often the quickest way to identify the sort of bird you're looking at. In fact, sometimes it's the only way. If a bird flies away before you can find it with the binoculars, or if it's dark against gleaming water, the outline is the only clue you've got. Silhouettes that are easily confused are shown here side by side.

Great Crested Grebe

Mallard

Coot

Canada Goose

Mute Swan

Cormorant

Diver

Lapwing

Sandpiper

Water Rail

Grey Heron

Crane

Stork

Herring Gull

Great Skua

Osprey

White-tailed
Sea Eagle

Peregrine Falcon

Marsh Harrier

Puffin

Razorbill

Guillemot

57

Photographing birds

Sea and freshwater birds are some of the easiest to catch on camera. They're often quite large and slow-moving, and less likely to fly off at the rustle of a rucksack. Here are some tips for getting a good shot:

• Get as close as you can by moving slowly and quietly.

• Start out with gulls, swans, ducks and geese. They let you get closer than small birds do.

• Scatter bread on the ground and keep out of sight to lure birds within range of your camera.

• If you're photographing a bird in flight, you'll get the best results at dawn or dusk. That's when the Sun's low and lights the bird from underneath.

• Don't restrict your pictures to single birds. Large flocks give some spectacular shots.

These gulls have perched long enough for an easy photo

Useful words

breeding season – the time of year when a pair of birds mate, build a nest and rear their young

colony – a group of birds of the same *species* nesting close together

courtship display – the way a bird behaves to attract a mate. Some birds show off their plumage; others put on a "display" in the air.

dabbling ducks – a group of ducks that stick their head underwater with their tail ends sticking up, to feed on water plants. This is known as upending.

diving ducks – a group of ducks which feed by diving for food underwater

drake – male duck

eclipse – the dull-coloured plumage of male ducks as they *moult* their feathers

habitat – a place where a *species* of bird normally lives

juvenile – a young bird which has left the nest and whose plumage is not yet the same as its parents'

migration – the regular movement of birds from one place to another

moult – when birds lose their old feathers and grow new ones. All birds moult at least once a year.

resident – a bird that remains all year in the area in which it nests

roost – when a bird sleeps; or a place where birds sleep

sawbill – a group of diving ducks with a saw-edged bill

species – a group of birds that all look alike and behave in the same way. For example, Herring Gull is the name of one species.

speculum – the bright coloured feathers in a duck's wing

wildfowl – a name for ducks, geese and swans

Scorecard

When you start spotting, you'll soon find that some birds are rarer than others. To give an idea how likely you are to see each kind, they're listed with a score.

Common species score 5 points and rare ones score 25. If you like, you can use the "Spotted" boxes to record where and when you saw them.

Species	Score	Spotted	Species	Score	Spotted
American Wigeon	25		Brent Goose (dark-bellied)	20	
Arctic Skua	20		Brent Goose (light-bellied)	20	
Arctic Tern	15		Canada Goose	5	
Avocet	25		Carolina Duck	15	
Barnacle Goose	20		Common Gull	10	
Bar-tailed Godwit	20		Common Sandpiper	15	
Bean Goose	25		Common Scoter	20	
Bewick's Swan	20		Common Tern	15	
Bittern	25		Coot	5	
Black Guillemot	20		Cormorant	10	
Black-headed Gull	5		Crane	25	
Black-necked Grebe	25		Curlew	15	
Black Stork	25		Dipper	15	
Black-tailed Godwit	20		Dunlin	10	
Black Tern	20		Eider	15	
Black-throated Diver	20		European White-fronted Goose	20	
Black-winged Stilt	25		Ferruginous Duck	25	
Blue-winged Teal	25		Fulmar	15	

Species	Score	Spotted	Species	Score	Spotted
Gadwall	20		Kingfisher	20	
Gannet	20		Kittiwake	15	
Garganey	25		Knot	15	
Goldeneye	20		Lapwing	10	
Golden Plover	15		Leach's Petrel	25	
Goosander	20		Lesser Black-backed Gull	10	
Great Black-backed Gull	15		Lesser White-fronted Goose	25	
Great Crested Grebe	15		Little Egret	25	
Greater Flamingo	25		Little Grebe	15	
Great Northern Diver	25		Little Ringed Plover	20	
Great Skua	20		Little Tern	20	
Great White Egret	25		Long-tailed Duck	20	
Greenland White-fronted Goose	20		Mallard	5	
Greenshank	15		Mandarin Duck	15	
Green-winged Teal	25		Manx Shearwater	20	
Grey Heron	10		Marbled Teal	25	
Greylag Goose	10		Marsh Harrier	25	
Grey Phalarope	25		Moorhen	5	
Grey Plover	15		Mute Swan	5	
Grey Wagtail	15		Night Heron	25	
Guillemot	15		Osprey	25	
Herring Gull	5		Oystercatcher	15	
Kentish Plover	25		Peregrine	20	
King Eider	25		Pink-footed Goose	20	

Species	Score	Spotted	Species	Score	Spotted
Pintail	20		Slavonian Grebe	20	
Pochard	15		Smew	25	
Puffin	20		Snipe	15	
Purple Heron	25		Snow Goose	25	
Purple Sandpiper	20		Spoonbill	20	
Razorbill	15		Spotted Redshank	15	
Red-breasted Goose	25		Squacco Heron	25	
Red-breasted Merganser	20		Storm Petrel	25	
Red-crested Pochard	25		Surf Scoter	25	
Red-necked Grebe	25		Teal	15	
Red-necked Phalarope	25		Tufted Duck	10	
Redshank	10		Turnstone	15	
Red-throated Diver	20		Velvet Scoter	20	
Reed Bunting	15		Water Rail	15	
Reed Warbler	15		Whimbrel	20	
Ringed Plover	15		White-headed Duck	25	
Ring-necked Duck	25		White Stork	25	
Ruddy Duck	20		White-tailed Sea Eagle	25	
Ruff	20		Whooper Swan	20	
Sanderling	15		Wigeon	15	
Sandwich Tern	20		Woodcock	15	
Scaup	20				
Sedge Warbler	15				
Shag	15				
Shelduck	15				
Shoveler	15				

Index

Edited by Simon Tudhope
Designed by Anne Sharples and Marc Maynard
Digital manipulation by Keith Furnival

Additional illustrations by Graham Allen, Dave Ashby, Bob Bampton,
John Barber, Derick Bown, Roger H Coggins, Denise Finney, Sheila Galbraith,
Christine Howes, Ian Jackson, Andy Martin, Annabel Milne, Robert Morton,
Tricia Newell, Richard Orr, Peter Stebbing, David Wright and others

PHOTO CREDITS: Cover © Edwin Giesbers / Foto Natura / Minden
Pictures / Getty Images; 1 © Tom Brakefield / CORBIS; 2 and 3 © David
Tipling / Alamy; 7 © Papilio / Alamy; 8 © DAVID TIPLING / naturepl.com;
56 © blickwinkel / Alamy

This edition first published in 2010 by Usborne Publishing Ltd,
83-85 Saffron Hill, London EC1N 8RT, England. www.usborne.com.
Copyright © 2010, 1985, 1979 Usborne Publishing Ltd.
The name Usborne and the devices 🎓 🎈 are Trade Marks of
Usborne Publishing Ltd.